Prison Segmentation for Startups Ideas

Rev. Mike Wanner

Copyright
Rev. Mike Wanner

October 20, 2017

Selected Images Used by License

Table Of Contents

Copyright 2

Table Of Contents 3

Introduction 4

1 - Defining Segmentation 5

2 - Appearances and Perspectives 7

3 - Impersonal Nature Of Prison 9

4 - The Complications of Tight Speace 11

5 - The Skills of Prisoners Inventory 13

6 - The Needs of Prisoners Inventory 15

7 - Space Possibilities 17

8 - Invitation To Prisoners 18

9 - Prisoner Segmentation Motivation 22

10 - Essential Services At The Startup 23

11 - Prison Community Can Do a Lot More 24

12 - Changing Your Mind Changes A Lot 25

13 - One Idea of Possibility 26

14 - But What About You? 28

15 - Thank You 29

16 - Don't Worry Ever 30

17 - Resource Books 31

18 - Angels Please Prayers 34

19 - Private Channeling 35

20 - Reverend Mike Wanner 36

Introduction

I have been writing about Segmentation and how it can help, but now it is time to define a startup process whereby a warden at a prison could project a no-cost way to begin.

The emphasis is on no cost because that is the only way to get a foothold in as many places as possible.

Please be mindful of the simplicity of not recreating the wheel. Organizations that choose to participate can serve the whole incarceration community well by creating multiple possibilities and opening networking efforts to share your plans and ideas with other facilities.

Sharing stimulates creativity, support, simplicity, and progress.

1 - Defining Segmentation

Segmentation is offered as a tool to help manage the complexity of the whole prison situation and provide a variety of little options that can make the impossible appear more manageable.

Rules and authorities that oversee the various facilities are real necessities, and there is no suggestion for them to be eliminated.

I want to offer some ideas here for consideration that will slice up impossibilities like a pizza.

Eating a whole pizza would be awkward and messy. Slicing up the pie into manageable slices makes it simple, less messy and quicker with less effort.

Fairness in this process must be apparent and will be crucial to acceptance. Equal treatment for all is much easier to discuss than constructive favoritism.

Segmentation may seem impractical in some facilities because of design differences, regulating authorities and geographical variables. All these challenges could be identified, analyzed and made somewhat more manageable with creative solutions.

I intend to fully root this book and all my others in the respect that each individual desires and deserves. Respect for many people is not given because the one who could offer it may lack the understanding of what the connection is and how one shows it to other people.

All too often people demand respect, and within that demand, they lack respect for the one who they wish to show it to them. They cannot give you what they do not have or see so show it to grow it and then give it to get it.

Giving and receiving are most compatible and abundant when you have a giver who expects nothing in return.

If there is nothing returned there is no problem. If there is something returned then the receiver who has already given may be blessed abundantly by the giver who had an abundance of something that the giver needed and never expected.

When I read about the prisons and the courts and the treatment of prisoners, I am always aware of the impersonal nature of the dialogue that I read. It is like; nobody wants to give, just receive.

In my experience, a little consideration goes a long way. I invite readers to self-test themselves for sensitivity to others.

A good reason to be sensitive and respectful is that it is the right thing to do. Another excellent reason to do it is that it can be much less stressful to all and much more productive for all.

2 - Appearances and Perspectives

Let's return to sensitivity and respect for a bit because they are crucial to interpersonal dynamics. The isolation of prison seems to be traumatizing to even the most hardened tough skinned macho dudes.

Isolation in prison can co-exist in space where there are many people close together. Prisoners can feel isolated from those who are close by because of uneasiness and lack of peaceful connection.

Giving comfort to others is a characteristic of a healthy individual who has a balanced, peaceful life. Prisoners can be close together in a dense space and still feel isolated.

The goal of incarceration is to keep those, who pose a threat to others, separate from those in the general community who may be victimized by the incarcerated.

Prisons are organized to fulfill this duty, and in many ways, they do that just as assigned.

The government has short-range goals, and long-range goals and both require resources which need to be managed and funded.

The responsibilities of government are many and complex, and there is a lot to be done besides managing and funding prisons.

Citizens of all ages and needs have to be served in a way that promotes peaceful coexistence and good order. Besides prisons, the government needs to fund, oversee and manage services like police, fire, roads, bridges, hospitals, trash collection, schools, municipal administration, emergency management and public health policies to name just a few. The government has a lot to do, and then they need to create taxes to support it all.

All these things are priorities that need to be managed so government must have an administration plan and administrators to run it all.

Prisons Wardens have all the needs and dynamics that people in the community need and they also have the overhead of hiring staff to serve and guard all the prisoners. They also have human interactions which can be much more problematic than the general community.

Prison budgets are tight so frills may be less than abundant. The bottom line is that prisons have too few dollars left to offer towards rehabilitating prisoners and that can be contra productive.

Prisons are not like businesses. Prisons do not want return customers but have too little resources to work with that can rehabilitate the customers they have.

The customers (prisoners) come back again and again and again. The taxpayers pay and pay and pay.

Let's change the way prisons cycle.

3 - Impersonal Nature Of Prison

The impersonal nature of prisons could be a much more problematic than many people may think. While disconnection may seem like freedom from criticism to some people, it also suppresses community participation because there is little pride to go around.

At the same time as there is an impersonal feeling, there is also a denseness that comes from the physical closeness even though there is not a feeling of bonding or connection.

Prisons are putting a lot of effort into further disconnection of prisoners as they cutoff frequency and sometimes availability of visitation. To me, this situation moves down the road in the wrong direction.

Segmentation can isolate prisoners enough, so they are less influenced by the impersonal nature of prisons now. Prisoners can find some peace and personal space and begin anew to reassess their options, self-worth, and value going forward.

We need to allow rehabilitation of prisoners by providing choices that can be ignored or chosen to help them put their life back together and be ready to reenter the community.

The reality now seems to be that there are at least three types of prisoner paths:

1. The ones who have given up because there is no hope of anything of value in their future.

2. The ones who will suffer through and make as good a life as they can out of what is left.
3. The ones who will survive and thrive regardless of all the challenges there are for them.

I hope there are more levels than I have written above but I share those with the hope that readers can grasp the need for the segmentation that I am proposing. There are probably mixed variations of some of the above categories, but I would like to see segmentation embraced to improve the experience for all prisoners regardless of sentence length or endless time.

Segmentation is about giving everybody a bit of relief and time to reassess. While that statement may sound old and familiar, my proposal is modified to bring real options for support, recognition, and encouragement.

While I believe that prisoners can do a lot for themselves with bits of opportunity to self-determine, I also know that teamwork is a most productive option. There are different kinds of collaboration.

While prisons could de-incentivize teamwork for security reasons, isolation does not promote rehabilitation. Hopefully, the day will come when prisoners have the will and the means to help themselves feel connected to society again.

Imagine if you will, adequately motivated prisoners are growing to the point where they start doing things they want to do to benefit the broader community.

4 - The Complications of Tight Space

Think back when you were in your childhood and lived in a house. Occupancy of the rooms would vary throughout the day as you went about your activities.

Different members would be in separate rooms at different times because everybody had the ability to relocate when the mood struck them. Prisoners do not have that choice, and that may be one of the reasons for some of the stress and tension that exists within today's prisons.

At home, if the music was too loud or not to your liking, you could quickly move to a different room or put on headphones and arrange for your ears to hear things that were more welcome. Prisoners have their freedom restricted, and that is the way things have to be to a significant degree.

In tight spaces with little ability to influence the things around them, prisoners can feel stress. Now stress is not something that is unusual because, in every community of free citizens, they are complaining about the stress in their lives.

Stress like everything in prison is complicated by the human density where people are always around. While the free citizens working in business complain about it also, when work is over they get to go home and relax in an environment that can offer them a retreat from the workplace intensity where they have more space to relax and more ability to control more of the circumstances of their situation.

After an evening of relaxation and a night of rest, free citizens can return to their workplace refreshed and ready to take on the challenges of each new day.

Prisoners get up in the morning still in close proximity to all those who have been so close and maybe even uncomfortably close to them. It is likely that prisoners do not get anywhere near as much rest and relaxation as a free citizen.

While I am not suggesting that there is anything wrong with a prison, I am suggesting that stressed out prisoners can be a lot more challenging to manage and supervise than most other people in the community would be.

When things happen in prison, reactivity could be intensified because there has been only minimal opportunity to rest and recuperate. Prison staff may be at a heightened risk because of the stress affecting prisoners.

The money to have stress free prisons does not exist, but I am hopeful that rethinking and cooperation can progress to a level that makes change possible, likely and cooperatively accomplished.

some readers may think that is unrealistic, but change only happens when it is believed possible. Another possible change maker could be saving money by eliminating conflicts.

I do not have the answers to all I am suggesting, but I do think the information is already available in the minds of prisoners and prison staff that could promote the right changes if they could work on developing a cooperative alignment.

5 - The Skills of Prisoners Inventory

There will be no funding for resources for Segmentation so a way to expedite the process would be to inventory the skills of prisoners and invite offers of participation. All should know from the outset that the capabilities offered will be considered, but there is no way to know if the skills proposed can be used until we have also inventoried the interests of prisoners.

Prisoners who have any of the following skills may be especially welcome:

1. Discussion Group Leadership
2. Hobby Group Leadership
3. Interest Groups of all Kinds
4. Skill Group Proficiency of all Kinds
5. Skill Group Leadership or Certifications
6. Job Development Leadership Group
7. Networking Group Proficiency
8. Self-Worth Group Leadership
9. Art Training Skills
10. Computer Group Leadership

11. Fear Release Group Leadership

12. Stress Release Group Leadership

13. Internal E-mail Group Proposals

14. External E-mail Group Proposals

15. Spiritual Direction Group Leadership

16. Alcohol Treatment Proficiency

17. Alcohol Treatment Coaching

18. Addictions Treatment Proficiency

19. Addictions Treatment Coaching

20. General Coaching and Monitoring

21. Mental Illness Coaching Credentials

22. Add other skills_____

23. Add other skills_____

24. Add other skills_____

25. Add other skills_____

26. Add other skills_____

6 - The Needs of Prisoners Inventory

There will be no funding for primary resources for Segmentation so after the inventory of prisoner skills as proposed in the last chapter; we will need to inventory the needs that prisoners identify. While all are invited to list their needs, the administration may find it necessary to decline, restrict, or further segment services available to any requested services in a way they determined to be fair, equitable and safe.

Prisoners are invited to list areas that could be helpful to them. Segmented services should not be considered as professional services which are part of the mandated services of their incarceration.

Professional services should be requested in the manner provided by the administration. Segmented services would be optional and always subject to the requirements of appropriate authorities.

Please indicate with a value of one (least) to five (highest) your interest level in any (up to five) of the added or listed services below:

___Discussion Group Participation

___Hobby Group Participation

___Interest Groups

___Skill Group Proficiency

___Job Development Group

___Networking Group

___Self-Worth Group

___Art Training

___Computer Group

___ Fear Release Group

___Stress Release Group

___Internal E-mail Group

___External E-mail Group

___Spiritual Direction

___Alcohol Treatment

___Addictions Treatment

___General Coaching

___Mental Illness General Support

___Other skills_____

___Other skills_____

7 - Space Possibilities

At night people sleep, and prisons may be quiet. In the daytime, there are a lot of people moving around in prisons to participate in their regular daily activity.

Every prison is different, and there are over 6,000 separate incarceration facilities in the United States, and every one may be a little different. The differences may be advantageous or complicate things depending on many factors.

The goal of segmentation is to use space in an optimal way so that space occupancy can be spread into as many places as possible at all times so that prisoners have as much space in which to live and move about throughout the day.

Earlier I wrote about access and safety and security and joint ventures and mental peace as part of the segmentation effort, and I would like to see all that considered and developed.

While waiting for all that to happen, I would encourage a gradual start-up of programs based on the skills inventory and prisoners needs as submitted from which the whole system can grow.

Creative discussions will be needed to reconfigure some space that can be well monitored but also somewhat private.

So let us talk about some bullet points that invite prisoners to apply for a segmentation experience whereby we can offer them a number of options that are different from the typical things that are provided now.

8 - Invitation To Prisoners

Adoption of the segmentation concept will involve a lot of details, and they will vary by each different facility. In order to continue to further the conversation and setup, I have drafted some paragraphs that could be added to or edited into the final document.

I start each paragraph with a - because I do not want my suggestions to be taken literally as fact but merely as component ideas which need integration in a thorough plan.

-Greeting to all residents, we would like to see if it might be possible to arrange some no-cost improvements in your home here. We realize that we are squeezed and want to work together to add some basic amenities that could enhance your time with us.

-Please understand that our budgets are already tight and in order to do the things we would like, we need to reallocate the resources that we have.

-It has been suggested to us that there may be some value in allowing some personal time that is not within the normal setup that you routinely expect.

-Participation is not required but would be suggested. The only rewards that we could offer are the authority to do what you request if it falls within our ability to authorize and we agree with your requests.

-We would like suggestions for both time blocks and activities that are reasonable extensions from which to grow different opportunities.

-One thing that could work is to add a bit of choice to your day, and we invite suggestions so your home here could be more comfortable.

-Eventually, we would like to use time around the clock where the diffusion of people provides niches of space that can be very peaceful for residents.

-Access to space as a 24-hour facility which used areas progressively developed to multiple uses. Working more like hospitals and Airports can shift a lot of things.

-The way to start would be one prison for one time for one prisoner in an authorized use of space that would never have happened before because it was never believed possible before.

-The right space use, motivations, and access controls could begin to progressively refit activities to allow reduced prison conflicts, increase correction officer safety, reduce medical costs incidental to conflicts, reduced lost corrections officer's time caused by being hurt scuffling with prisoners.

-The forms suggest an idea could accumulate feedback which could help target future efforts. Each facility could look for prisoners who would like to experience program variations.

-Declare to prisoners that you would like to offer regular change segmentation time. This encounter would be one time only initial opportunities for volunteers to spend time away from their typical patterns.

-The segment periods could be of any length that made sense to the facility and the prisoners and could offer some no-cost perks that could feel like freedom choices for the prisoners.

-Perhaps it could be nothing more than an opportunity to watch TV with no one else around.

1. Have a quiet time without other prisoners or guards.
2. Have a quiet writing block to work in their notebook.
3. Have clearly defined time to correspond with family.
4. Have clearly defined time to Skype with a spouse.
5. Have a clearly defined time to message administration.

-Key to this experience would be privileges that offer an incentive to cooperate in prison upgrades that do not cost the system but provide the prisoner value and motivation towards future cooperation.

-Cancellation and substitution should be allowable in case there are situations within the prison that would cause the prisoner to worry that participation would send a wrong message and make them somewhat vulnerable.

-The priority with this whole effort would be to give and receive a pattern of courtesy and kindness that could benefit everybody in the prison community and later the general population and especially the prisoners, prison staff, taxpayers and all the families of them all.

-Creative thinking voluntary alone time can lighten the thought of busy minds and promote peaceful silence that can provide unlimited potential for years to come.

-The future can be diminishing for prison occupancy and bright for prison staff and prisoners as the heaviness lifts and recognition of rethinking, realigning and repurposing blossoms into rapid rehabilitations that all are supported by, delighted with and fulfilled by their participation.

-The hope is that little bits of free time can prepare prisoners for the fresh, purposeful insight that can smooth reentry to the community in as simple a process as possible.

-Existing Correction officers would then have more time to help prisoners who are willing to work towards rehabilitation.

9 - Prisoner Segmentation Motivation

Prisoners may typically have a feeling of having limited freedom of choice. Segmentation may help.

Listing feelings could be helpful to prisoners to decide about segmentation. What constrictions do you have because of the way things are?

Many questions to consider asking yourself:

> Are you intimidated by the present living arrangements?
> Do you feel isolated or supported?
> Are there things that you would like the space to do?
> Would you like to change some things up?

All taxpayers are affected by the costs of prisons. All citizens are worthy of as much freedom as their behavior allows.

Collateral damage for the children of prisoners due to the incarceration of the parent is just not fair. Children need their parents and segmentation can help with the healing preparation.

I invite prisoners to think of the whole facility on a 24-hour schedule and them being free on a B shift or C shift to go to places with peace, purpose, and possibility.

Be aware of safety because you can travel in a different flow than people who are not friendly to you. More free movement is the beginning. Get ready to GET OUT and STAY OUT!

10 - Essential Services At The Startup

In the beginning, little steps can be started to develop the ideas expressed in the segmentation books. During these early setups, consideration could be given towards simple substitute services like bag lunches or Continental Breakfasts to allow prisoners to start to get the flavor of all that could be possible.

So there could be NO room for misunderstanding, it would be helpful to the entire community if there was a letter of intent initiated for each program at startup. The emphasis on startup would be to do it right the first time so that it can be done again and again and again.

The hope with this system would be the benefit of additional space and freedom which could ultimately be instrumental in making a case for more creative changes to the institutional control systems.

The simplest way to move forward can be the teamwork that seems lacking in prison. Ideally, we can move towards a scenario where the underprivileged of yesterday can begin to become the insurers of privileges for those who without their efforts would be doomed to the injustices of the past.

Teamwork and justice and freedom while the goals of the Formation of this country, may have been lost to many. Let us now use the devastation of incarceration to identify and change the problems of yesteryear and create a new bounty of possibilities now. Let us all seek peace as we build on the foundation of freedom that has nurtured our predecessors in the country that we treasure.

11 - Prison Community Can Do a Lot More

Prison, Prisoners, Prison staff and taxpayers can all do a lot more with a lot less. We can grow teamwork and tenacity, and we can upscale the lives of all who help us.

Helping each other is the key to survive and thrive in a free society. Prison seems to create a ceiling to freedom but no limit to stress, anxiety, and confusion.

We can break through limitations if we have enough motivation and support. We can focus our collective energies in new ways that will create opportunities for success for us all.

Prison residents and staff can each enhance the lives of each other if they can discipline themselves enough to listen and consider. The key to unlocking success is understanding the needs of each other and gifting others with kindness.

Life is like the story of a perspective of heaven and hell. I know not the author or I would give credit.

The story shows the same picture of a place of bounty where all sit at a table of opportunity epitomized by luscious fruit and vegetables and delicacies of all kinds. The problem in both pictures is that the utensils are attached to the hands of those at the table in a way that makes it impossible for each person to feed themselves.

Hell has all at the table starving as they struggle to get nourishment. Heaven has all people thriving because they each take turns in feeding each other. Which table would you choose? If you make a mistake, you can change your mind.

12 - Changing Your Mind Changes A Lot

Your mind can filter things out or allow them into your life. It would be my recommendation that you begin to reassess the choices of the past that set the limits of what you have now.

You are a powerful being even if you have been broken by your life circumstances or any of the events that occurred since your birth. The sturdy little tool that can help you begin a new journey of personal discovery is a kindness.

Be kind first to yourself and soothe the pain that you know. Next look metaphorically for the burrs under your saddle that impact on the horse you ride.

As you treat yourself more kindly and spread the impact of your kindness to other beings on the planet, your state of mind will morph into a potential that you have not even dreamed possible. That new vision of possibility can be a bit much, and it can take you into a feeling of vulnerability that is new and fresh.

While that may sound challenging, the reality is that it may be an unknown quantity that you can assess, evaluate and develop into a future that you might like. Think positive. See opportunities. Be confident. Turn your life around. Change your mind and your life together.

13 - One Idea of Possibility

I delight in telling the story of my niece to many people. It precedes the idea of "I think I can." It is the concept of I might be able to after all.

I am blessed to have a couple of delightful nieces, and they are like many of us in that they have had their challenges. My oldest niece is now a Nurse Practitioner with a Pediatric Specialty.

Earlier on in her life, her potential was not so clear to her as she graduated high school with very few career possibilities in mind. Like so many children her parents had divorced, and this left a shadow of confusion over the path for her life.

She was not thinking like the let's go to college crowd but more like the let's find a job and get to work thinkers. Then she talked about her future with my mother, and her concept of the future shifted.

She did not know nor did any of us in the family that my mother had been making steady deposits towards her education. I never knew the amount that was available nor is that important.

The information for my niece was tremendous as it launched a concept of possibility that shifted everything. Suddenly, my nieces' outlook on life was enhanced, and she thought that her life could be more and that her grandmother cared enough to help make that possible.

The idea that there was possibility grabbed hold of her mind and rekindled her dreams. She started to pursue optimistic ideas and succeeded.

The potential led to a higher blessing as her chosen career field nursing was understaffed, and there were incentive programs for possible students. The perfect plan she found was across the river in New Jersey, and the deal was that graduates would be offered a job within a certain number of years or their remaining tuition bill would be canceled.

When she graduated, the employment market had shifted, and there were too many nurses for the available jobs. They did not have a job for her, and they canceled her tuition balance.

She found a job elsewhere within a reasonable time, and her life became enhanced because of a single idea of possibility. Thank You, God!

I remain hopeful that subtle little shifts in operations can change the possibilities for prisoners just like my niece's whole life has been modified by a conversation with my mother, her grandmother.

14 - But What About You?

The truth may be that your worst and only enemy has been yourself. I have been one who saw reality in a limited way, but I did get real in all aspects of my life.

The patterns of your past are able to be shifted, and the only ruler of that reality is you. If you would like your days ahead to be better than the days in your past, I invite you to shift your thinking and begin a journey of seeing, believing, requesting and manifesting a future that is increasingly gratifying.

If you believe in yourself, there can be extraordinary JOY ahead. What has worked for me is to focus on helping others and ignoring the things that previously bothered me.

When you are ready, you can extend a hand of kindness to others. Maybe the force of the universe who matters more than anything else, will notice your new sparkle and support your efforts even more.

May all who read this be blessed, AND SO IT IS!

Mike

15 - Thank You

For Considering These Ideas

16 - Don't Worry Ever

It Does Not Help Prayer Still Does!

Resource: http://www.Create-A-Prayer.com

17 - Resource Books

Books by Rev. Mike at www.Amazon.com

Veterans Healing Six Pack
1. *Trauma Healing Options for VA Hospitals: Help for Veterans to Own Their Healing and their future.*
2. *Trauma Healing Action Steps for Veterans: Help to Start Healing*
3. *Trauma Healing Action Steps for Veterans: Empowerment*
4. *Trauma Healing Action Steps for Veterans: Forgiveness*
5. *Trauma Healing Action Steps for Veterans: Thought Freedom*
6. *Tea For Veterans: Welcome One Home*

PTSD Power Pack:
1. *The PTSD Project: Turn Pain To Power*
2. *PTSD & Soul Retrieval: Putting One Back Together*
3. *PTSD & The Purple PAD: Calling all Scientists and PTSD Patients*

Angel Raphael Speaks Volume 1: Take Courage! God Has Healing in Store for You!
Angel Raphael Speaks Volume 2: Take Courage! God Has Healing in Store for You!
Angel Raphael Speaks Volume 3: Take Courage! God Has Healing in Store for You!
Angel Raphael Speaks Volume 4: Angels, Addicts, Alcoholics & Prisoners – Oh Yeah!
Angel Raphael Speaks Volume 5: Prisoners Caring for Alcoholics - Australia In Miniature Projects Intro
Angel Raphael Speaks Volume 6: Prisoners Caring for Addicts - Australia In Miniature For Addicts
Reiki Journaling from Japan
Reiki Is Alive: God's Great Gift
Four Parts to Healing
Distant Healing: We Are All Connected

Stress Release Energy Work: How To Cope
Does Reiki Love Heal Cancer?
Group Consciousness
Salute To Philadelphia VA Medical Center: Thank You
Reiki Transcript for Reiki 2 & 3 Channels: Dr. Usui Is That You?
God Bless Kindle & Amazon
Puppies Are Different From People
If Your Dog Dies
Toy Guns Are Obsolete
Great Spirit Made Children With Red Skin: AND
The Cage of Fear: Is Not Locked
God Made Children Red, Yellow, Brown, Black & White: Greet Each Child With Kindness
Emergency Medical Kindness In The Cradle Of Liberty: Big City - Cracked Bell
Angels Are Always Around Addicts and Addicts: Help Is Near Now! Invite It In!
Angels Are Always Around Addicts and Alcoholics: Volume 2 - Tools To Help Re-Light Your Life
Prison Jobs Now: Providing Care For Addicts And Addicts
Controlled Care Communities Concept
Prison Possibilities Dialogue Series: Concept
Prison Possibilities Dialogue Series: Volume 2, 3, 4, 5 Dialogues
Prison Possibilities Voluntary Exile
Prison Possibilities Corrections Coaches
Prison Possibilities For Mexicans: Is A Boat Better Than A Wall?
Prison Possibilities Family Time: A Reason to Thrive!
Prison Genius Pool: "So Much Genius In Jail."
Prison Possibilities Access Control: Prisoner Access by Request
Prisoner's Lawyers Can Save The American Economy: Make A Buck Doing It & Be Thanked!
Prisoner Family Talks, Days, Stays & Vacations: Connecting Helps Healing
Prisoner Writing Projects: Write To Heal, Start Over & Reconnect

Prison Cell Clearing & Blessing: Clear Entities, Chase Ghosts, and & Create Sacred Space
Prisoner Professors: Show You Are Aware Create Change With Care
Prison Reiki? Maybe Someday? A Gateway To Help Heal Prisons & America?
Judges and An Angel Rule On Possibilities: We Can Cut Sentences & Prison Costs
Ideas For Prison Wardens: Leadership Is Not Easy
Solitary Community: Could Community Support Cut Costs and Issues?
Prison Project Communications Team: Communications Can Change Lives
Motivating & Empowering Prisoners? Invite Prisoners To Find Their Motivation
Prison Segmentation For Safety, And Sanity, Security, Peace, and Space
Prison Segmentation For Security
Dowsing for Prisoners; Answers from Above
Ex-Prisoner Possibilities With Real Estate Investors
Prison Segmentation For Mental Peace
Prison Segmentation for Joint Ventures

Little Books at Kindle.com by Rev. Mike:
English Medical History Questionnaire For Non-English Speakers
English Language Helper For Non-English Speakers
Wise Wonderful Women Are The Well Of The Family
Answers for Test & Research: Dowsing Power
Crisis? Reiki! Baby? Reiki!
Bible References For Healing
Angel Raphael Speaks – Prisons
Angel Raphael Speaks – Veterans
The Saint Off Interstate 95

18 - Angels Please Prayers

Addict's

Angels of Healing Selected
Help Me to Stay Directed
Come To Me From The Sky
I Am Ready to Succeed Not Try
If I Don't Invite You In
I Might Not Win
I Have Been Lost For Too Long
Help Me To Stay Strong

Alcoholic's

Angels of Healing On High
Help Me to Stay Dry
Come To Me From The Sky
I Am Ready to Succeed Not Try
If I Don't Invite You In
I Might Not Win
I Have Been Lost For Too Long
Help Me To Stay Strong

From

http://AngelRaphaelSpeaks.com/AAAAAAA/

19 - Private Channeling

Angel Raphael Speaks a series of free messages that are channeled through Reverend Mike Wanner for the Highest good and Highest Healing of all concerned.

Many questions arise about Reverend Mike doing private channeling, and he does help with that so e-mail him.

Reverend Mike is available worldwide as a psychic channel, emotional release facilitator, spiritual energy practitioner & teacher, and public speaker. He looks forward to meeting you soon!

Email - mikewann@voicenet.com 215-342-1270 PRIVATE SPIRITUAL READINGS/channelings or Spiritual Healing Sessions: Telephone or in person. Rev. Mike is available for private, one-on-one intuitive sessions with you, his Guide Family, and your Guides. He helps by offering clarity on emotional situations about your life, your purpose, your spirituality, and the release of stuffed emotions and cellular memory.
Connect to the love of your Guides today!
Contact Rev. Mike for an appointment.

Sessions available:

Spiritual Readings	Angel Channeling
Distant Reiki Healing	Remote Clearing of Stuffed Emotions
Distant Clearing Cellular Memory	Distant Clearing Energy Blockages
+Remote Clearing of the Chakras	Customized needs

Mastermind dowsing responses to yes/no direction finding questions.

Rev. Mike is a facilitator of healing. He brings you and the Divine together so that you can align with the Divine and have a great time and a great life. All healing is between you and God, as it should be. Go ahead and start without Rev. Mike. Visit his prayer site http://www.Create-A-Prayer.com. Take the first step NOW.

20 - Reverend Mike Wanner

Rev. Mike Wanner started his Metaphysical and Ministerial studies with Reiki in 1993 and had studied seven styles of Reiki in the U.S., Japan, Canada, Denmark and Australia. He is certified to teach. He became certified to teach Integrated Energy Therapy in 1999 and co-taught the first IET class of the new Millennium. Mike began dowsing in 2001.

Ordained as a Metaphysical Minister of the International Metaphysical Ministry and an Interfaith Minister of the Circle of Miracles Ministry, Rev. Mike practices and teaches spiritual energy therapies in the Philadelphia Area.

Rev. Mike holds ministerial degrees from the University of Metaphysics and the University of Sedona. He is a Pastoral Care Associate of Aria - Frankford Hospital. He taught at the National Academy of Massage Therapy and Health Sciences.

Rev. Mike was a faculty member of the Medical Mission Sister's Center for Human Integration's School of Integrated Body/Mind Therapies in Fox Chase, Philadelphia, PA for twelve years.

Rev. Mike is licensed by the teaching of Intuitional Metaphysics to practice Spiritual Healing and Scientific Prayer. Mike is also a Prayer therapist.

Rev. Mike was elected in 2007 to the status of "Fellow of the American Institute of Stress."

In 2008, Rev. Mike became a practitioner of Coincidental Recognition as he incorporated the CoRe System into his spiritual healing practice.

In 2009, Rev. Mike trademarked a new healing process called Quantum Quatro! Subtle Energy System Support®.

In 2011, Rev. Mike joined the outreach program known as the Health Advantage Group.

In 2012, Rev. Mike became a Certified Professional Coach by The Master Coaching Academy and Joined the Personal Empowerment Group.

Before his Metaphysical, Ministerial and Coaching studies, Rev. Mike worked for Sears Roebuck and Co. while in High School and after graduation, until he joined the U. S. Air Force in 1965. He returned to Sears from Vietnam in 1969 and stayed until 1978. His final Sears assignment was as an efficiency expert in Methods - Operational Research and Development.

He volunteered with Burholme Emergency Medical Services from 1969 and is still a Life Member and Board of Directors Member. He started a private ambulance company in 1975 and worked professionally in the field until 2001 when he devoted his full attention to real estate investing, healing, coaching, and writing.

May All Who Read This Be Blessed
AND SO IT IS!